Get to Work with **Science** and **Technology**

The Wild World of a
Zoo Vet

by Ruth Owen

Consultant:
Ghislaine Sayers BVSc. MSc WAH MRCVS
Head of Veterinary Services, Paignton Zoo Environmental Park, Devon, England

Published in 2016 by Ruby Tuesday Books Ltd.

Copyright © 2016 Ruby Tuesday Books Ltd.

Editor: Mark J. Sachner
Designer: Emma Randall
Production: John Lingham

Photo Credits:
Alamy: 18; Richard Austin/Rex: 4–5, 6–7, 16–17, 26–27; Corbis: 11 (bottom), 15 (bottom), 20 (right), 24; FLPA: Cover, 8, 13 (top), 19, 20 (left); Getty Images: 9, 21; Press Association Images: 28–29; Rex Features: 22–23; Science Photo Library: 13 (bottom), 15 (top); Shutterstock: Cover, 10 (top), 12, 14, 25, 30.

Library of Congress Control Number: 2015907062

ISBN 978-1-910549-34-6

Printed and published in the United States of America

For further information including rights and permissions requests, please contact our Customer Service Department at 877-337-8577.

Contents

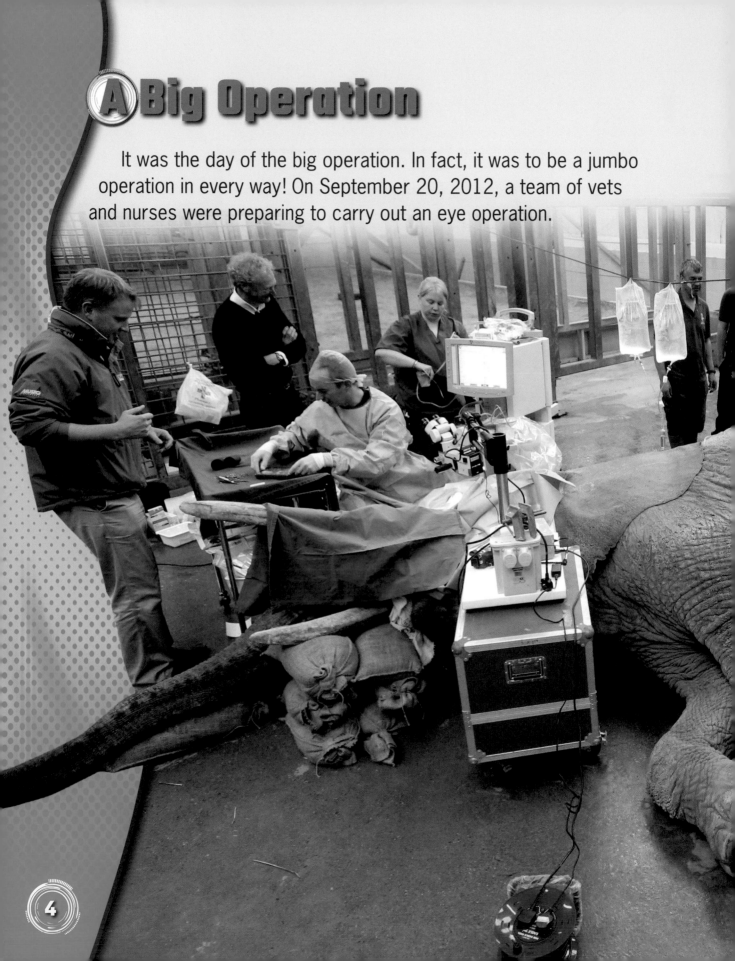

A Big Operation

It was the day of the big operation. In fact, it was to be a jumbo operation in every way! On September 20, 2012, a team of vets and nurses were preparing to carry out an eye operation.

The patient was Duchess, a 42-year-old African elephant. Duchess had already had her right eye removed. Now her left eye had **cataracts**. This condition makes the see-through lens in an eye turn cloudy. Poor Duchess could no longer see from her remaining eye.

The operation took place in Duchess's enclosure at Paignton Zoo, in Devon, England.

As Duchess's keepers quietly talked to her to reassure her, zoo vet Ghislaine Sayers injected the huge elephant with a powerful dose of **general anesthetic**. Slowly, Duchess sank to her knees and then rolled onto her side. When the medical team was sure she was asleep, they quickly went to work.

A Team Effort for Duchess

As Duchess the elephant slept, veterinary **ophthalmologist** Jim Carter began the operation. An ophthalmologist is a vet or doctor who is an expert at treating eye diseases and problems.

To treat Duchess's cataracts, Jim used an ultrasonic handpiece. This tool makes tiny vibrations. The vibrations broke up the cataracts, or cloudy parts of the eye's lens. Then Jim used another tool to suck the damaged tissue from the eye.

During the operation, vets and nurses monitored Duchess's heartbeat and breathing. Each time she breathed out, they measured the amount of carbon dioxide gas in her breath. This told the team if Duchess was breathing normally or needed help.

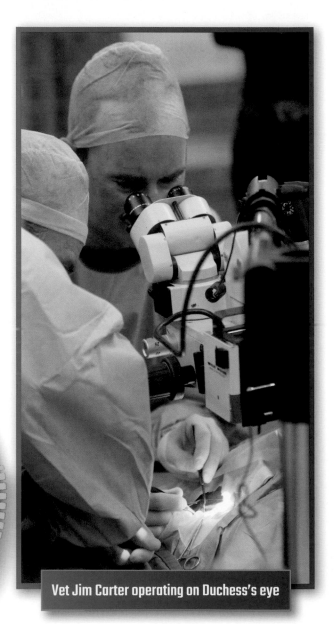

Vet Jim Carter operating on Duchess's eye

The vets gave Duchess oxygen and anesthetic gases through her trunk.

Trunk

After nearly three hours, the operation was complete. Duchess was given another injection. This one contained a chemical to wake her up.

As the elephant wobbled to her feet, everyone breathed a sigh of relief. Thanks to the skills of the veterinary team, not only had Duchess survived the operation, but now she would be able to see again!

Duchess gently examines her eye after the operation.

All in a Day's Work

Just like the vets who treat our pet cats and dogs, zoo vets spend their days caring for animals. A zoo vet may have more than 2,000 animals to look after. The biggest might be an elephant. The smallest could be an endangered rain forest frog or spider.

Zoo vets usually work as part of a team with other vets and veterinary nurses. The team works in the zoo's examination room and out in the animals' enclosures.

Zoo vets deal with emergencies and perform operations. They also carry out lots of day-to-day tasks. These include trimming hooves, **microchipping** animals, and giving the animals **vaccinations** to protect them from diseases.

A zoo vet gives a pelican a vaccination to protect it against bird flu.

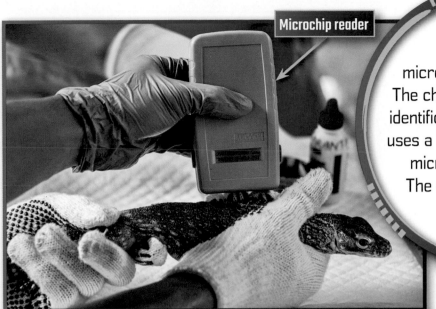

Microchip reader

Many zoo animals have a microchip under their skin. The chip contains the animal's identification number. A zoo vet uses a large needle to inject the microchip into an animal. The chip can then be read with a microchip reader.

This baby Komodo dragon has just been fitted with a microchip. The vet is checking the chip with a microchip reader.

A team of vets uses saws and power sanders to trim an elephant's toenails.

Solving a Piggy Problem

Being a zoo vet is all about using good science skills to solve problems. So what type of problem might a zoo vet face? Here's an example.

A red river hog

Question

Two red river hogs share an enclosure. Two new hogs come to live at the zoo. Each day the zookeepers give the hogs enough food for four animals. The two original hogs start to look thin, however.

Why are the hogs losing weight?

Research

The vet observes the animals to see if they seem ill or in pain. The vet weighs the hogs and checks them against a chart that gives scores for certain body conditions.

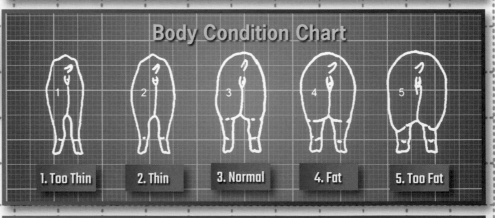

Body Condition Chart

1. Too Thin 2. Thin 3. Normal 4. Fat 5. Too Fat

Form a Hypothesis

The vet's research shows that the two hogs are thin but not unwell. The vet wonders whether the new hogs might be bullying the thin hogs and stealing their food.

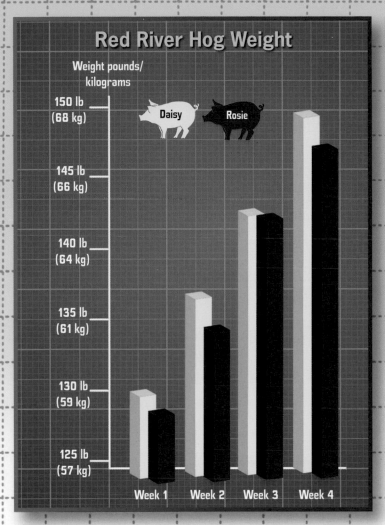

Red River Hog Weight

Weight pounds/kilograms

Daisy   Rosie

	Week 1	Week 2	Week 3	Week 4

150 lb (68 kg)
145 lb (66 kg)
140 lb (64 kg)
135 lb (61 kg)
130 lb (59 kg)
125 lb (57 kg)

The Test
The zoo vet asks the hogs' keepers to feed the two thin hogs away from their greedy housemates. Once a week, the vet weighs the thin hogs.

Analyzing the Data
After four weeks, the weight data shows that the thin hogs are now gaining weight.

Results
The two new hogs were stealing the thin hogs' food. Problem solved!

Scales

Zoo animals are trained by their keepers to climb onto scales to be weighed. Once an animal is on the scales, it is rewarded with a food treat.

Problem Solving with Poop

It may sound gross, but examining dung, or poop, is all part of a zoo vet's job.

Many animals have **parasites**, such as roundworms, in their stomachs. The worms lay their eggs in an animal's stomach. Then the eggs are passed out when the animal poops. If an animal has too many worms, it can become sick.

To test for parasitic worms, a keeper collects samples of dung. Then, the zoo vet examines the dung under a **microscope**.

In some enclosures it can be tricky to know whose poop is whose. If just one animal needs a dung test, that animal is fed food mixed with edible glitter—the kind that's used for decorating cupcakes. Once some sparkly poop appears, the keeper knows that's the stuff for testing!

Rhino dung

Keepers collect dung from an animal for three days to have the best chance of finding parasites in the samples.

A vet examines a dung sample under a microscope.

The vet looks for **microscopic** worm eggs and **larvae**. If there are lots of eggs and larvae, it means the animal has too many worms.

The zoo vet might give the animal a worming injection to kill off the parasites, or some medicine mixed into its food.

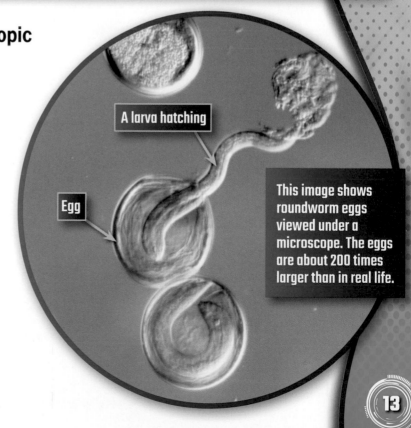

A larva hatching

Egg

This image shows roundworm eggs viewed under a microscope. The eggs are about 200 times larger than in real life.

Taking a Blood Test

Doing a blood test is another way to check for illnesses. Paignton Zoo's vet, Ghislaine Sayers, explains how this is done:

> One of our cheetahs had a small wound on her leg. She seemed less active than normal, and she was not eating. I thought the wound might have caused an infection, so I decided to do a blood test.
>
> The cheetah had been trained to stand close to her enclosure fence with her tail through an opening. Using a needle and syringe, I drew some blood from the cheetah's tail. Once I had taken the sample, the cheetah's keeper gave her a food reward. Then the blood sample was sent to a **laboratory** to be tested.

Needle

Syringe

At the lab, a scientist examined the blood under a microscope. The scientist saw there were more white blood cells than normal. Some of these white cells attack and destroy **bacteria** in an animal or person's body. The white blood cells had increased to fight off an infection caused by bacteria.

My diagnosis was correct, so I gave the cheetah **antibiotics** to treat the infection.

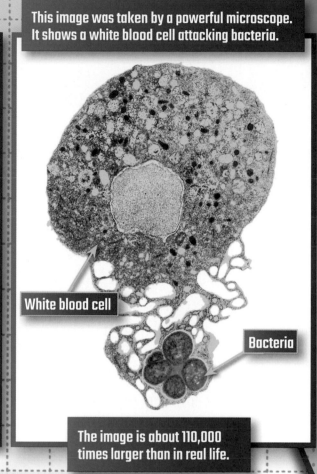

This image was taken by a powerful microscope. It shows a white blood cell attacking bacteria.

White blood cell

Bacteria

The image is about 110,000 times larger than in real life.

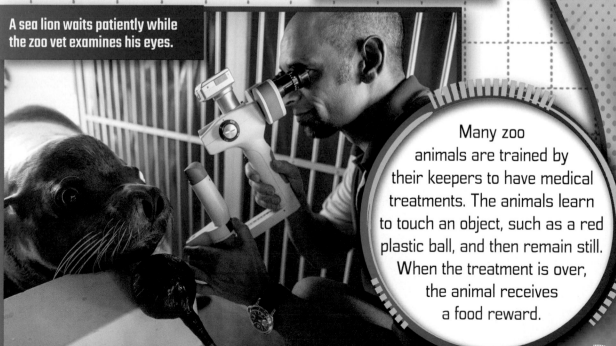

A sea lion waits patiently while the zoo vet examines his eyes.

Many zoo animals are trained by their keepers to have medical treatments. The animals learn to touch an object, such as a red plastic ball, and then remain still. When the treatment is over, the animal receives a food reward.

A Crash Helmet for a Tortoise

Some problems faced by zoo vets can be solved with just a little creative thinking.

One day, a giant tortoise at Paignton Zoo suffered a bad wound and ended up with a large hole in his shell. Zoo vet Ghislaine cleaned the wound with an **antiseptic** liquid to remove any dirt and kill any bacteria. Then Ghislaine applied **dressings** to the wound.

It's not possible, however, to stitch up a hole in a shell. So a member of the zoo's maintenance team made a section of fake shell from fiberglass. Then Ghislaine used duct tape to hold the fake shell in place.

The tortoise's shell would grow back in about 18 months. Until then, he would wear his new crash helmet!

Fake shell

Zoo vet Ghislaine Sayers

Ghislaine duct tapes the fake shell to the tortoise's real shell.

Zoo vets sometimes have to treat animals that are wounded in fights. Animals fight over food, nesting areas, or the best sunbathing spots. Male animals also fight over females.

Giant tortoise

Getting Up Close with Wild Patients

Zoo vets often have to get close to potentially dangerous animals.

To safely do this, a vet may anesthetize an animal with a dart gun. From outside the animal's enclosure, the vet shoots a dart into the animal. When the needle part of the dart pierces the animal's skin, anesthetic pumps from the needle. Within a few minutes, the animal is asleep.

A vet using a dart gun to anesthetize a tiger

A cartridge of carbon dioxide gas is attached to a dart gun. When a vet pulls the gun's trigger, the gas forces the dart from the gun into the animal.

An anesthetic dart in an elephant's skin

Zoo vets practice shooting dart guns. They must be good shots as animals quickly become scared or panicked. Also, a vet must dart an animal in an area where there is lots of muscle, such as its shoulder or bottom. The vet must avoid hitting nerves, blood vessels, the animal's eyes, or small, delicate bones.

No animal likes to be hit with a dart. A chimpanzee, however, may become very angry and throw the dart back at the vet! So after darting a chimp, the vet quickly moves away from the enclosure.

Time for a Check-Up

One of the reasons an animal may be anesthetized is for a check-up. Older animals especially need regular health checks.

The vet begins by asking an animal's keeper lots of questions about its behavior and day-to-day life. For example, is it eating normally? Does it sometimes have wet fur around its mouth? This could mean the animal is dribbling because its teeth are causing pain.

Next, every part of the animal is examined, including its eyes, mouth, nose, skin, hair, or feathers.

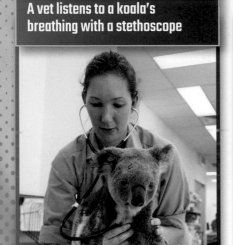

A vet listens to a koala's breathing with a stethoscope

A vet photographs a jaguar's teeth. The photos are kept as a visual record.

The vet listens to the animal's heart with a **stethoscope** to make sure the animal's heartbeat is normal. The vet also listens for how the air is flowing through the animal's lungs. An X-ray machine may be used to check the animal's bones and joints.

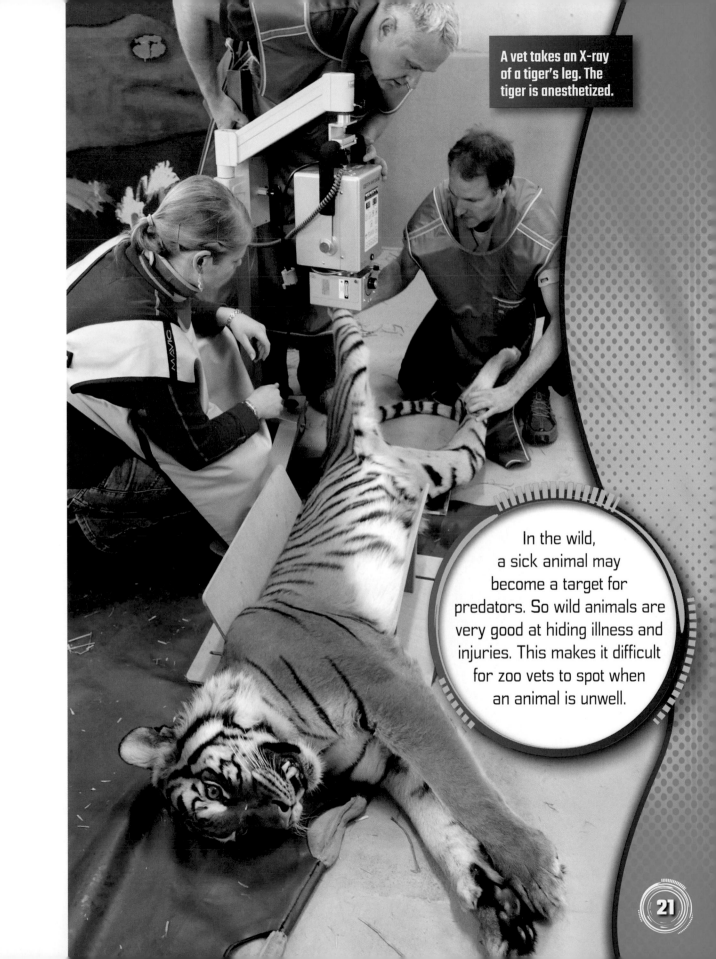

A vet takes an X-ray of a tiger's leg. The tiger is anesthetized.

In the wild, a sick animal may become a target for predators. So wild animals are very good at hiding illness and injuries. This makes it difficult for zoo vets to spot when an animal is unwell.

Tiny Socks and Paws with Pins

A behind-the-scenes peek into a zoo's veterinary center can sometimes reveal a few surprises. At Paignton Zoo in England, you might see a lion that looks like a pin cushion and a monkey wearing odd stripy socks!

When an animal is under anesthetic, its body gets cold. It loses heat through its extremities, such as hands and feet. Ghislaine Sayers and her team came up with a cute but practical solution. The animal's feet or hands are wrapped in bubblewrap and then covered with socks.

A brown spider monkey's hands stay warm and cozy as it undergoes an operation.

Where do the socks come from? Zoo staff members often find socks lost by babies or small children in the zoo grounds. These tiny socks are just right for keeping a monkey's hands and feet warm.

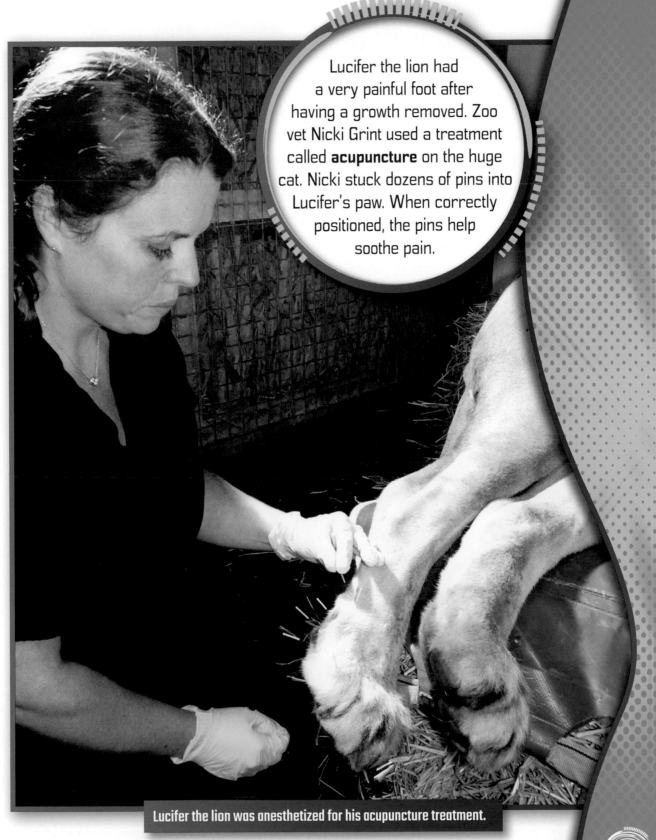

Lucifer the lion had a very painful foot after having a growth removed. Zoo vet Nicki Grint used a treatment called **acupuncture** on the huge cat. Nicki stuck dozens of pins into Lucifer's paw. When correctly positioned, the pins help soothe pain.

Lucifer the lion was anesthetized for his acupuncture treatment.

Zoo Vet Detective Work

Sometimes a zoo animal dies suddenly. It's important that the zoo vet finds out why it died. For example, the animal might have a disease that could spread to other animals in the zoo. To discover the cause of death, the zoo vet carries out a **postmortem**. This is a detailed examination of the animal's dead body.

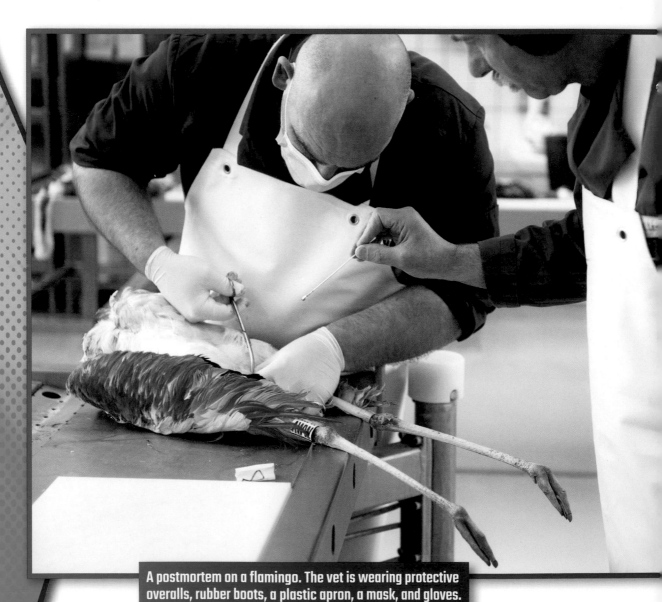

A postmortem on a flamingo. The vet is wearing protective overalls, rubber boots, a plastic apron, a mask, and gloves.

The body is weighed, measured, and photographed. The vet checks for any bruises, wounds, or skin diseases. Then X-rays are taken of the body to check for any damage to bones.

Finally, the vet cuts the body open. One by one, the vet removes and examines organs such as the heart, lungs, stomach, and liver.

At the end of the postmortem, the vet writes a report. The report records all the vet's observations and the reason for the animal's death.

An X-ray of a rattlesnake taken for a postmortem.

Saving Endangered Frogs

A very important part of a zoo vet's job is to help protect endangered animals.

Around the world, hundreds of **species** of frogs are in danger of extinction. People have cut down the rain forests where many frogs live. People have also allowed chemicals and other pollution to contaminate rivers and ponds.

Every frog species around the world is threatened by a fast-spreading, deadly disease. The disease is caused by a type of fungus called chytrid.

The zookeepers and veterinary team at Paignton Zoo are helping to save frogs. They breed frogs, such as the critically endangered golden mantella frog.

Members of the Paignton Zoo team study frog diseases. They also study frog habitats and how frogs live. This research is passed onto **conservationists** who help protect frogs in the wild.

Paignton Zoo's frogs are kept in a bio-secure unit. This means they are protected from diseases and the outside world. Before working with the frogs, the keepers and vets must change into clean, contamination-free overalls.

A golden mantella frog

Saying Goodbye to Old Friends

Around the world, zoos are breeding endangered animals. Zoos work together to match up animals with partners for breeding. Once a good match is made, one of the animal pair must move from its old home to be with its new mate.

Before a zoo animal moves, a vet must examine it to make sure it is healthy. The vet also tests the animal's dung and blood to make sure it has no diseases. When a new animal arrives at a zoo, the vet carries out the same checks.

Zoo vet Colin Scott gives white rhino Mazumba a final health check before she begins the journey to her new home.

At a large zoo, there may be animals leaving and new ones arriving every month. Saying goodbye to old animal friends, and welcoming new ones, is all part of a zoo vet's work.

A zoo vet must be sure an animal does not have a disease that could spread to animals in its new home. The animal must also be healthy enough to make a long, stressful journey.

Safe inside her crate, Mazumba is ready to move from Scotland to the Netherlands.

Get to Work as a Zoo Vet

Q&A

What subjects should I study?
Biology, chemistry, physics, and math. At a college or university, you will study veterinary science, or veterinary medicine and surgery.

How can I get experience with animals?
Try volunteering at stables, farms, or animal shelters. Veterinary clinics often offer work experience, too.

When does a zoo vet work?
The vets in a team take turns being on duty. You will need to work nights, weekends, and holidays.

Is being a zoo vet dangerous?
You will work with powerful animals that can kick and crush you, bite and scratch—including some animals with venomous bites, and birds with long, sharp beaks. Zoo vets are trained to be super careful at all times.

Do zoo vets have to do paperwork?
Yes! And lots of it. Every time a vet treats an animal, he or she must carefully record all the details. Zoo vets also have to order supplies and fill out paperwork for animals that are moving from one zoo to another.

What's the hardest part of the job?
A vet is a scientist, and the zoo's animals are not pets. All zoo vets, however, get attached to their animals, and they feel sad when an animal dies.

Design a Zoo Enclosure

Zookeepers, vets, and engineers work as a team to design and build enclosures for zoo animals. Try designing a safe, natural, interesting enclosure for a zoo animal.

1. Choose an animal—it can be as big or as small as you wish.
2. Research the animal in books or online. Find out about its physical capabilities and behavior, its everyday needs, how it lives in the wild, and its natural habitat.
3. Make a map or plan of the enclosure that shows all the features of the animal's new home.

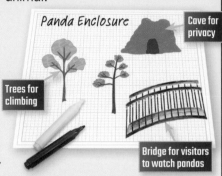

Panda Enclosure

Cave for privacy

Trees for climbing

Bridge for visitors to watch pandas

When working on your enclosure design, think about these questions:

- What size is the enclosure? How many animals will live there?
- Can the animal climb? How high or far can it jump? How will the design stop the animal from escaping?
- Where will the public viewing areas be? Does the enclosure have places where the animal can have privacy?
- Are there places where keepers and vets can safely interact with the animal?
- What is the weather like at the zoo? Is it hotter, colder, wetter, or drier than the animal's natural habitat? What can you do to create natural conditions for the animal?
- Does the animal need trees for climbing or a pool? What features does the enclosure provide to stop the animal from getting bored?

Dog Breath Experiment

How does exercise affect a dog's respiration rate?

Try your animal handling and research skills with this experiment. How many breaths does a dog take in one minute? If the dog exercises, will its respiration, or breathing rate, change?

To download the instructions for the experiment, go to:
www.rubytuesdaybooks.com/dogbreath

You can work with your own dog, or with a friend or family member's pet.

Glossary

acupuncture (AK-yoo-puhnk-chur)
An ancient medical treatment from China in which long, thin needles are inserted into the skin at particular points.

antibiotics (an-tih-bye-OT-iks)
Medicines, such as injections or pills, that kill or stop the growth of the bacteria that cause infections.

antiseptic (an-tih-SEP-tik)
Able to kill off bacteria.

bacteria (bac-TIHR-ee-uh)
Microscopic living things. Some bacteria are helpful, while others can cause disease.

cataracts (KAT-uh-rakts)
Cloudy areas in the lens of an eye that make it difficult to see.

conservationist (kon-sur-VAY-shuhn-ist)
A person who does work to protect wild animals, plants, and natural habitats.

dressings (DRESS-ingz)
Materials such as bandages or band-aids that are used to cover a wound.

general anesthetic
(JEN-ur-uhl an-iss-THET-ik)
A chemical that is injected into or is breathed in by a person or animal. It makes patients become unconscious and stops them from feeling pain.

laboratory (LA-bruh-tor-ee)
A room or building where there is equipment that can be used to carry out experiments and other scientific studies.

larvae (LAR-vee)
The young of some animals. A larva usually looks like a worm.

microchipping (MYE-kroh-chip-ing)
Injecting a tiny device, the size of a grain of rice, into an animal. The microchip contains information about the animal that can be read by a microchip reader.

microscope (MIKE-ruh-skope)
A tool or machine that is used to see things that are too small to see with the eyes alone.

microscopic (mye-kroh-SKOP-ik)
Only visible when viewed through a microscope.

ophthalmologist (op-thuh-MOL-uh-jist)
A doctor or vet who specializes in treating eye problems.

parasite (PA-ruh-site)
A living thing that lives on and gets its food from another living thing.

postmortem (pohst-MOR-tuhm)
An in-depth examination of a dead body to find out why an animal or person died.

species (SPEE-sheez)
Different types of living things. The members of an animal species look alike and can produce young together.

stethoscope (STETH-uh-skope)
A medical instrument used for listening to sounds from inside an animal or person's body.

vaccination (vak-suh-NAY-shuhn)
A substance that is injected into an animal or person to give protection against a disease.

Index

Read More

Owen, Ruth. *Zoologists and Ecologists (Out Of The Lab: Extreme Jobs in Science)*. New York: Rosen Publishing (2014).

Thomas, William David. *Veterinarian (Cool Careers: Helping Careers)*. New York: Gareth Stevens Publishing (2009).

Learn More Online

To learn more about zoo vets, go to:
www.rubytuesdaybooks.com/zoovet